Felicitas Vogler World of Light

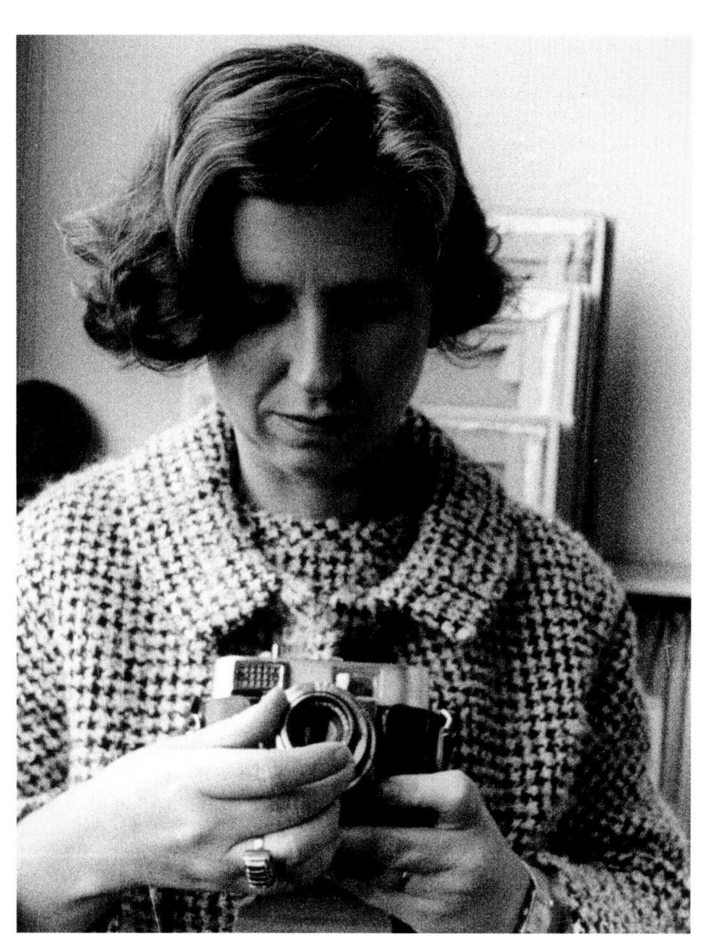

Patrick Elliott

FELICITAS VOGLER
WORLD OF LIGHT

National Galleries of Scotland
Edinburgh · 2006

Published by the Trustees of the National
Galleries of Scotland 2006 for the exhibition
Felicitas Vogler: World of Light held at the
Scottish National Gallery of Modern Art,
Edinburgh from 6 May to 9 July 2006.

Text © The Trustees of the National
Galleries of Scotland
Works © Felicitas Vogler

ISBN 1 903278 80 5 (978 1 903278 80 2)

Designed and typeset by Dalrymple
Copy photography by Antonia Reeve
Printed in Belgium by Die Keure

Front cover: *Namib Desert, Namibia,* 1973
Frontispiece: Hans Hartung *Felicitas Vogler,* 1968
Back cover: *Kyoto, Tenryu-Ji,* 1985

Foreword

The Scottish National Gallery of Modern Art always enjoyed a good relationship with Ben Nicholson, buying two of his works in the early 1960s as soon as they were finished. We are delighted to be able to continue and extend that relationship through this book and exhibition of photographs by Felicitas Vogler. Nicholson and Vogler were married in 1957, and it was from about that time that she began to work seriously as a photographer, concentrating in particular on the landscape. A major book on her work, *Felicitas Vogler: The Quiet Eye*, was published in 1969. In 1973 her first retrospective exhibition opened at the Institute of Contemporary Arts in London and subsequently toured Britain; her work was acquired by the Victoria & Albert Museum.

Initially her photography was confined to Europe but from the 1970s she travelled more widely, to China, Tibet, Japan, New Zealand and elsewhere. Although exhibitions of Vogler's photographs were held in Cambridge and London in the 1990s, this is the first publication in English on her work for more than thirty years, and the exhibition includes many works never previously seen in Britain. We would like to thank Felicitas Vogler for her support in making this publication and exhibition possible.

JOHN LEIGHTON
Director-General, National Galleries of Scotland

RICHARD CALVOCORESSI
Director, Scottish National Gallery of Modern Art

Felicitas Vogler: World of Light

When Felicitas Vogler says that she is not particularly interested in photography, what she means is that she is not interested in cameras, zoom lenses, aperture settings and darkrooms; she does not even mind if a photograph is a little out of focus. What really matters to her is how the photograph expresses a feeling, and through it, the personality of the photographer. In an essay written for the Swiss cultural journal *Du* in 1960 she stated: 'I would dare to assert that a great deal can be learnt about a photographer from his pictures, and not merely about his momentary state of mind, but about his character and mentality.'[1] The artist Ben Nicholson, whom she married in 1957, said something similar: 'When I draw an Italian cathedral I don't draw its architecture, but the feeling it gives me.'[2] It is that business of trying to capture a feeling, and trying to communicate that feeling to others, that lies at the heart of Vogler's photography.

Born in Berlin, Vogler was interested in the arts from an early age: her father, a keen amateur photographer, gave her a camera when she was eight. Her grandfather was an amateur painter and owned an impressive library of art books, which provided her with her art education. Vogler's interests were (and remain) very broad, giving her a striking array of career choices. A chance meeting sparked off a passionate interest in astrology and mythology, which she studied in Munich; she also studied in Freiburg and Vienna. Simultaneously, she began a PhD in psychology at Munich University. She completed her doctorate in 1950 and began working for Austrian radio in Salzburg, conducting research for arts programmes focusing on literature, music, philosophy and psychology. She was especially interested in Zen Buddhism and in Indian and Chinese philosophy and religion, steering a number of programmes in this direction. Apart from working in Salzburg, she also lived in Munich, researching literary programmes for German radio.

In 1955 Vogler helped with the organisation of a major international writers' congress in Vienna. She formed friendships with some of the British and Indian delegates and this led, the following year, to her first visit to London. By this time, her interest in India was such that she had determined to spend a year there, travelling and studying for a few months in an ashram. In May 1957 she visited London again, primarily to organise her trip to India. She took the opportunity to research a programme for Bavarian radio about the Cornish landscape, having been inspired by the letters Katherine Mansfield had written from Zennor, at the tip of Cornwall. A friend suggested she also visit St Ives and interview the various artists who had settled there. Vogler was interested in abstract art and the idea intrigued her.

In the first few days in St Ives she met Peter Lanyon, Bryan Wynter, Patrick Heron, Roger Hilton, Barbara Hepworth and Bernard Leach. Hepworth, who had separated from Ben Nicholson some six years earlier, thought that Vogler should meet Nicholson, the most celebrated but also the most reclusive of the St Ives artists. She telephoned him, explained that Vogler was no ordinary journalist, and arranged a brief visit that Friday morning. The half-hour meeting turned into a five hour conversation. Nicholson also insisted on driving her around the Cornish landscape over the next two days. Although Vogler enjoyed his company, she had no inkling that his feelings ran deeper. On the Monday, as planned, she set off for Wales to stay with friends, her mind still set on India. But a letter from Nicholson indicated

that he was keen to escape St Ives for a while, and Vogler's friends suggested that he should join them for a few days. It soon transpired that Nicholson's interest was centred on Vogler, not Wales: 'He swept me off my feet' she recalls. They were married at a London registry office, just six weeks after their first meeting.

The icy winter weather and the claustrophobic social life in St Ives soon proved oppressive and they considered moving abroad. Paris and the Côte d'Azur were possibilities, but she suggested the Ticino, the Italian-speaking part of Switzerland. To her surprise, he knew the area – as a young man, he had spent time in nearby Milan, where he had fallen in love with a German governess. In the early 1920s he had returned to the area with his first wife, Winifred Nicholson, and they had even bought a house in Castagnola. So in April 1958 Vogler and Nicholson moved to Switzerland, renting a house before buying a plot of land with breathtaking views of Lake Maggiore, just outside the village of Brissago, near Locarno. They had a house built and moved in during April 1961. Jean Arp, Julius Bissier and Italo Valenti were neighbours who became good friends.

Until this point Vogler had considered photography to be a hobby, but with Nicholson's support and encouragement her interest deepened. They took trips into the Swiss and Italian countryside, and while he drew, she took photographs. Her photographs were first published in exhibition catalogues of Nicholson's work produced by the Lienhard gallery in Zurich in 1959 and 1960. This was followed in December 1960 with the publication of her essay 'Travels with Pencil and Camera' in *Du* magazine. Trips to the Greek Islands in 1959 and the early 1960s led to some of her best-known photographs, of parched landscapes and of whitewashed buildings silhouetted against azure skies. There is an obvious parallel with Nicholson's work, in the way in which landscape and architecture are treated almost as components in an abstract, geometric composition. This was not a matter of influence, rather it was an interest which they shared when they met, and which brought them together. She was attracted to ordinary, undramatic sights which have a quiet rhythm about them: green trees in a green field; the patterns of graffiti on a wall; upturned boats. They suggest a pure, gentle vision, as if the world were being seen for the first time.

Throughout this time she was also working professionally as an astrologer. Photography and astrology might appear to be unrelated activities, but for Vogler they are two sides of the same coin: they demonstrate a deep curiosity about the natural world and its underlying forces and structures. She is not religious in the traditional sense, but one can see that her interest in the planet Earth and the stars is part of a single world view.

Nicholson's move to Switzerland had served to heighten his international profile and underline his position as one of the greatest living European artists. Vogler's reputation also increased and was cemented in 1969 with the staging in Zurich of her first exhibition and the publication of her book *Felicitas Vogler: The Quiet Eye* (published a few months earlier in German as *Lichte Welt* or *World of Light*). This large-format book included photographs taken in Italy, Portugal and Greece. The landscape architect Geoffrey Jellicoe wrote a short, introductory text, while Nicholson provided a more personal commentary. The English title came from Wordsworth's poem *A Poet's Epitaph*: 'In common things that round us lie / Some random truths he can impart, / The harvest of a quiet eye / That broods and sleeps on his own heart.' Vogler particularly liked the line and used it for a number of subsequent exhibitions, including her first retrospective, held at the Institute of Contemporary Arts in London in 1973. 'The quiet eye' captures the essence of her work, the way in which her photographs elevate small moments into something grand and profound. As Nicholson commented: 'The landscape or architecture which F photoes do, like a painting, reveal *what is in her mind*. It is just this point which interests me – that by one pressing of a lever so much of the mind of the photographer is revealed.'[3] The book prompted an equally lucid note of approval from the great furniture designer Marcel Breuer: 'The photographs are beautiful, the colours non-synthetic, non-chemical, like the painter's palette. But Felicitas Vogler's work is not imitative of painting. Despite its air, its content, its poetry, and its dart direct to the soul, it is photography, information, a reflection of reality – a true and noble mastering of a technique. No tricks, simple, even humble.'[4]

Over time Nicholson became more and more ruminative and isolated in Switzerland. This was largely self-inflicted: his obsession with his working routine had led to a drawbridge mentality in which friends were discouraged from visiting and phone calls went unanswered. What he was missing above all was the English language. Although he spoke French and Italian well enough, he could not joke or express himself with the same subtlety and depth as he could in his native tongue. He spent an increasing amount of time writing to English friends, but this was not enough, and in 1971 he decided to return home. Vogler, however, preferred to stay in Switzerland: the marriage had lost its joie de vivre and the climate and surroundings in Ticino suited her. Nicholson settled in Cambridgeshire. Vogler helped him move and their parting was amicable; she visited him regularly in the following years.

Nicholson's leaving led to a new departure in Vogler's photography. No longer required to tend to his needs, she had the opportunity to voyage further afield and concentrate on her own work. Her travels took her to Namibia and South Africa in four consecutive years between 1973 and 1976; Ladakh and Kashmir in 1976; Bhutan and Sikkim in 1977. Some of the trips coincided with exhibitions (in South Africa, for example) while on others she joined small groups which explored the country by road. She travelled to Egypt in 1980 and China and Tibet later that year; Japan on four occasions between 1985 and 2004; the Hindu Kush and the Silk Road in 1989 (not long after the first primitive roads had been laid for army use); New Zealand in 1990 and 1991; and Russia no less than seven times. These remote locations brought about a new kind of imagery in her work – an imagery that was grand and dramatic in contrast to the more manicured landscapes of her earlier European work. But no matter where she was photographing, she always sought to capture the particular spirit of the place. As she has stated: 'first there is the excitement one feels on arriving in new places, an excitement which is – I like to think – the encounter of one's own being with the special beauty of the place concerned, touched off by an infinite receptivity for the ephemeral and un-recapturable accord of form, colour and light. In the best of cases it is even more: a sense of being lifted into another dimension, where one perceives something that is not only this house, this field or mountain, but this spirit also, that creates it, moves it, and breathes through it.'[5]

[1] 'Travels with Pencil and Camera', *Du*, December 1960.

[2] Ibid.

[3] Letter, 23 February 1969, to Geoffrey Jellicoe, quoted in *Felicitas Vogler: The Quiet Eye*, London, 1969, p.23.

[4] Letter, 30 October 1970, collection Felicitas Vogler.

[5] 'Travels with Pencil and Camera', *Du*, December 1960.

PATRICK ELLIOTT

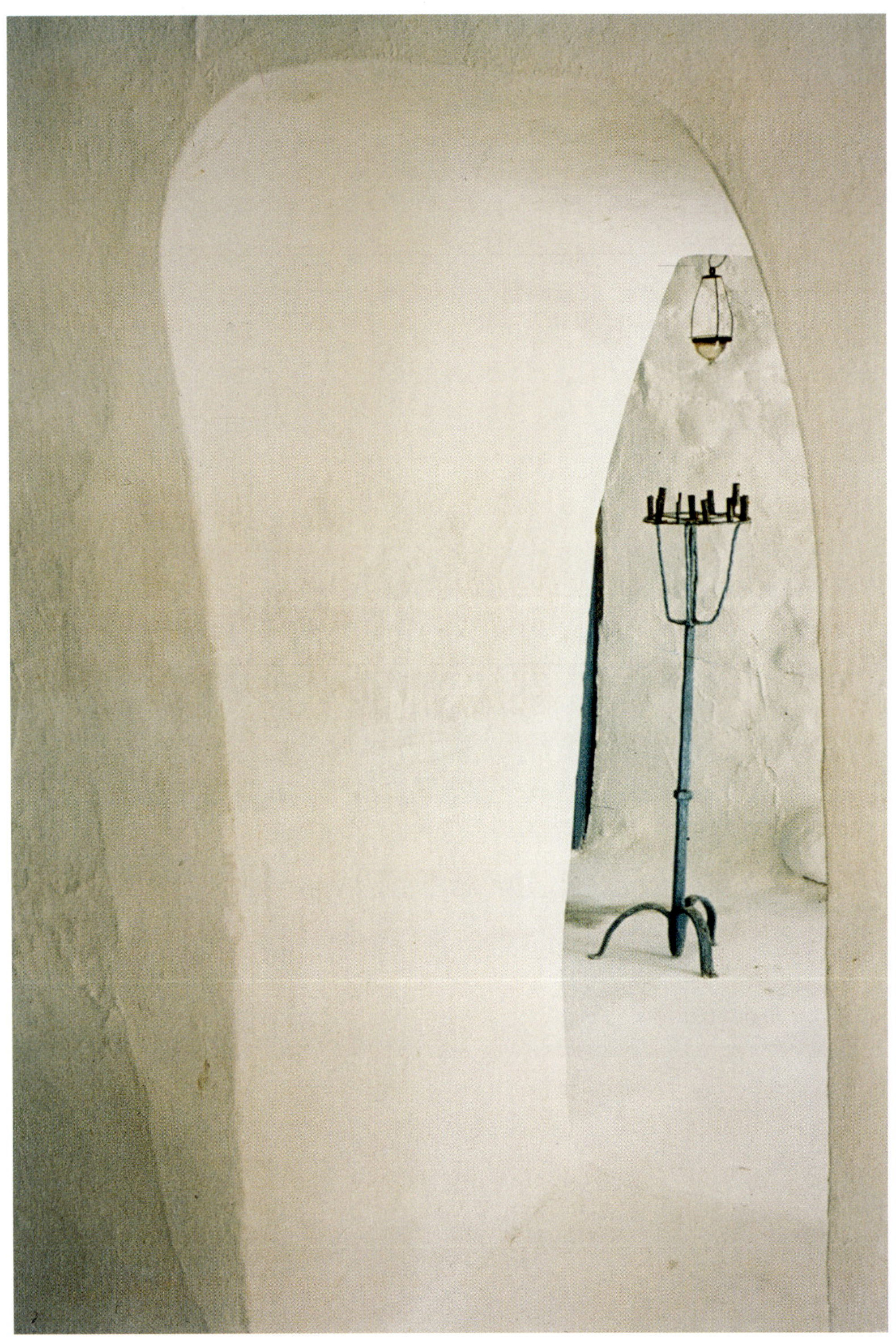

Chapel with Candelabra, Mykonos 1959

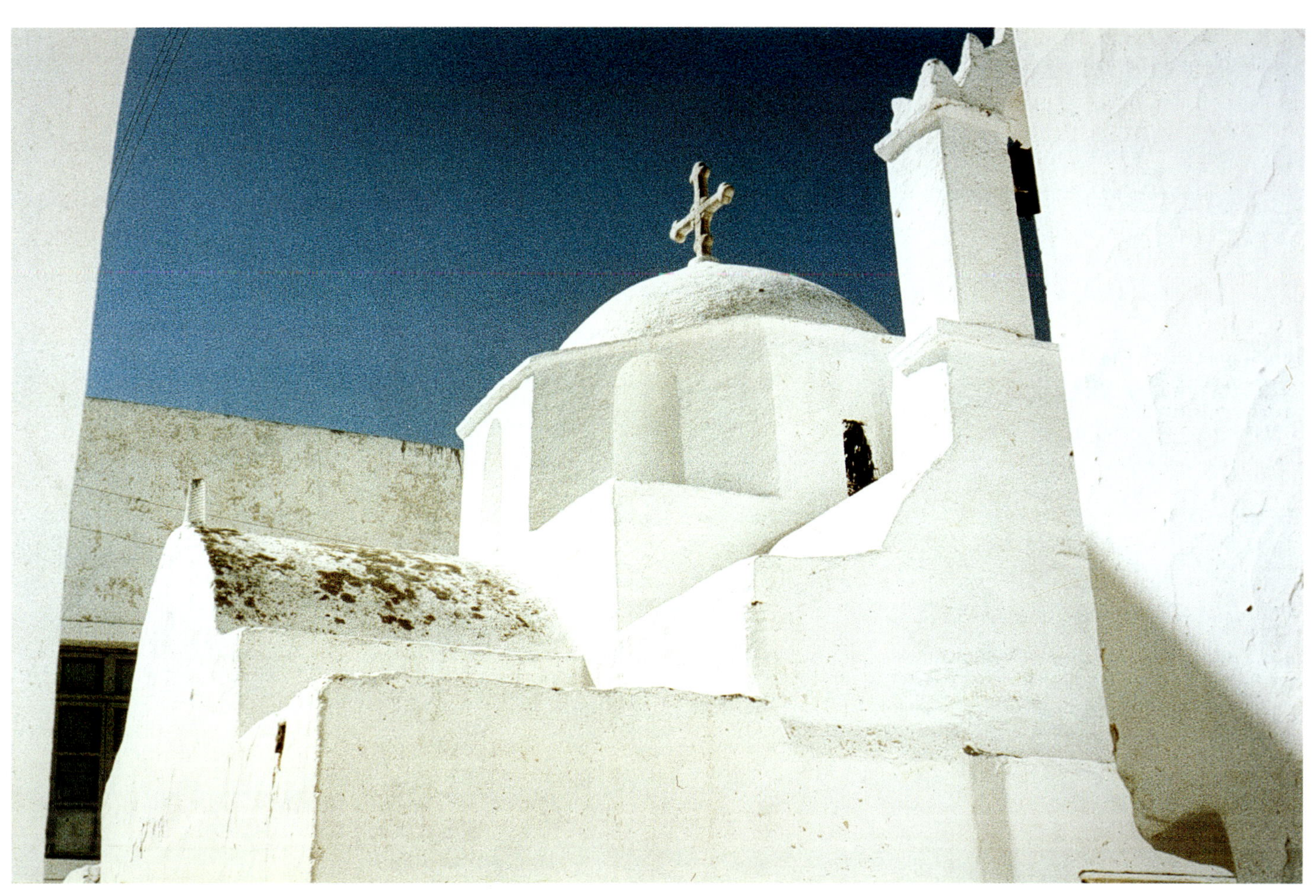

Paros 1959

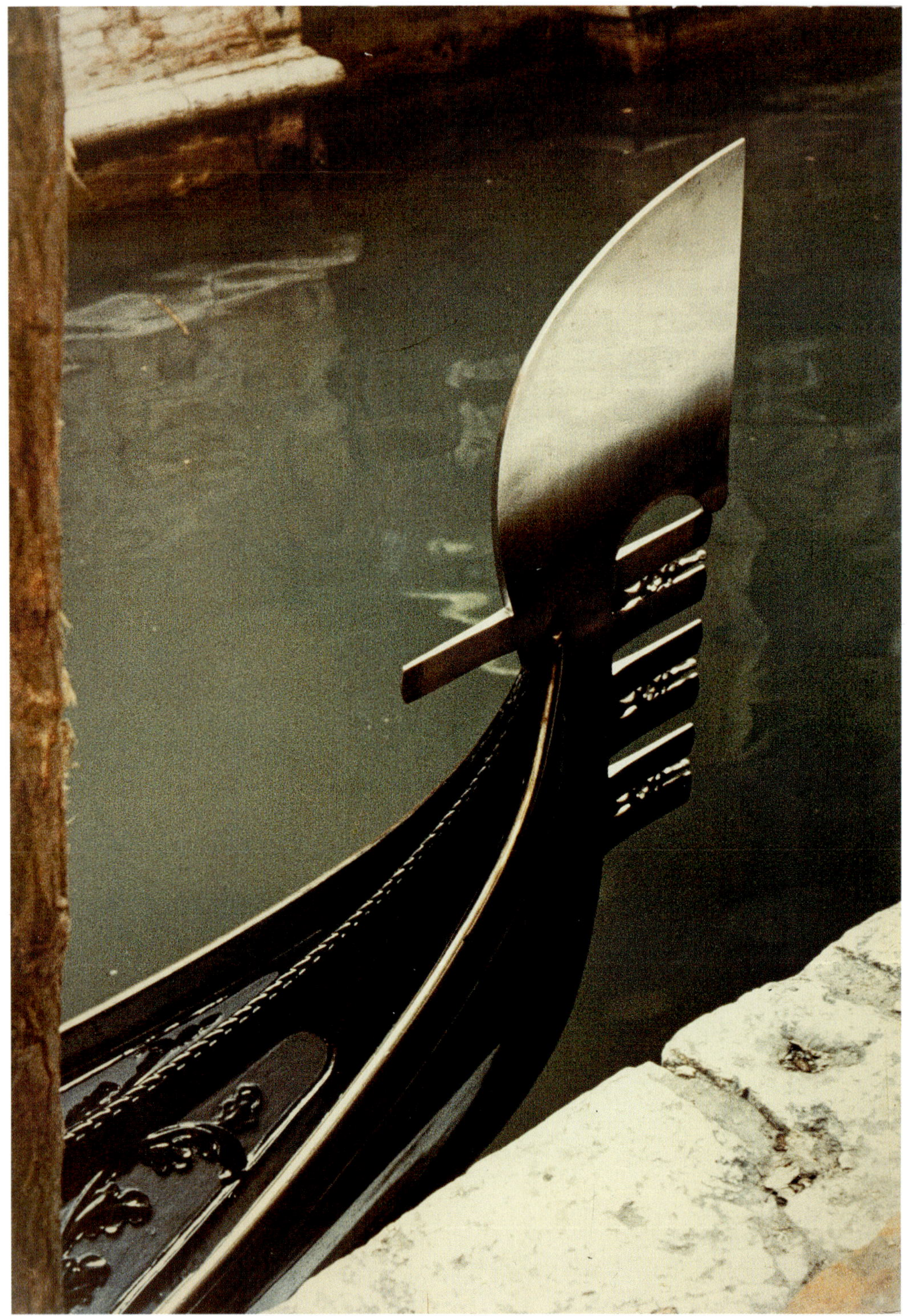

Venice 1966

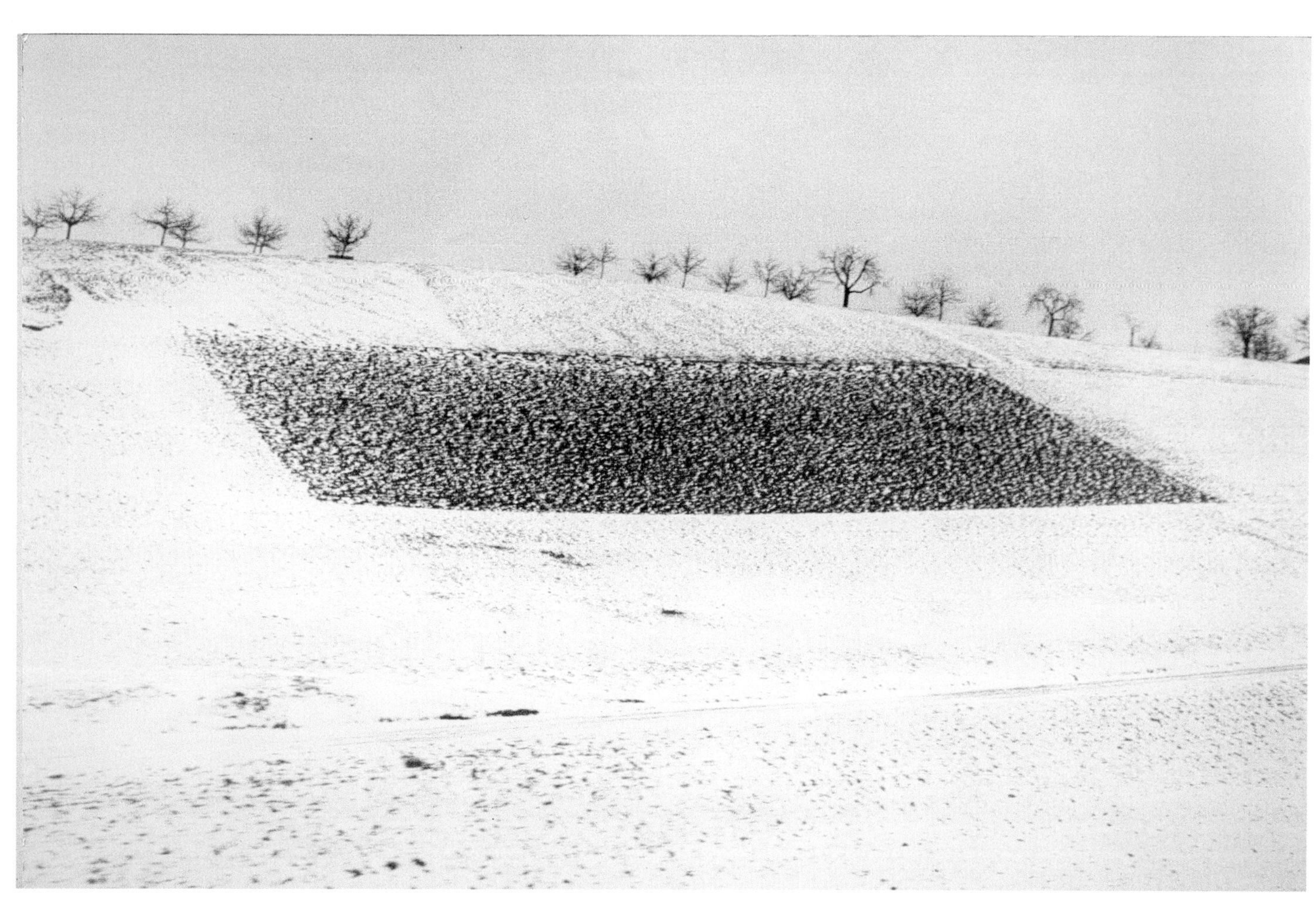

Emmental – Morning Train 1967

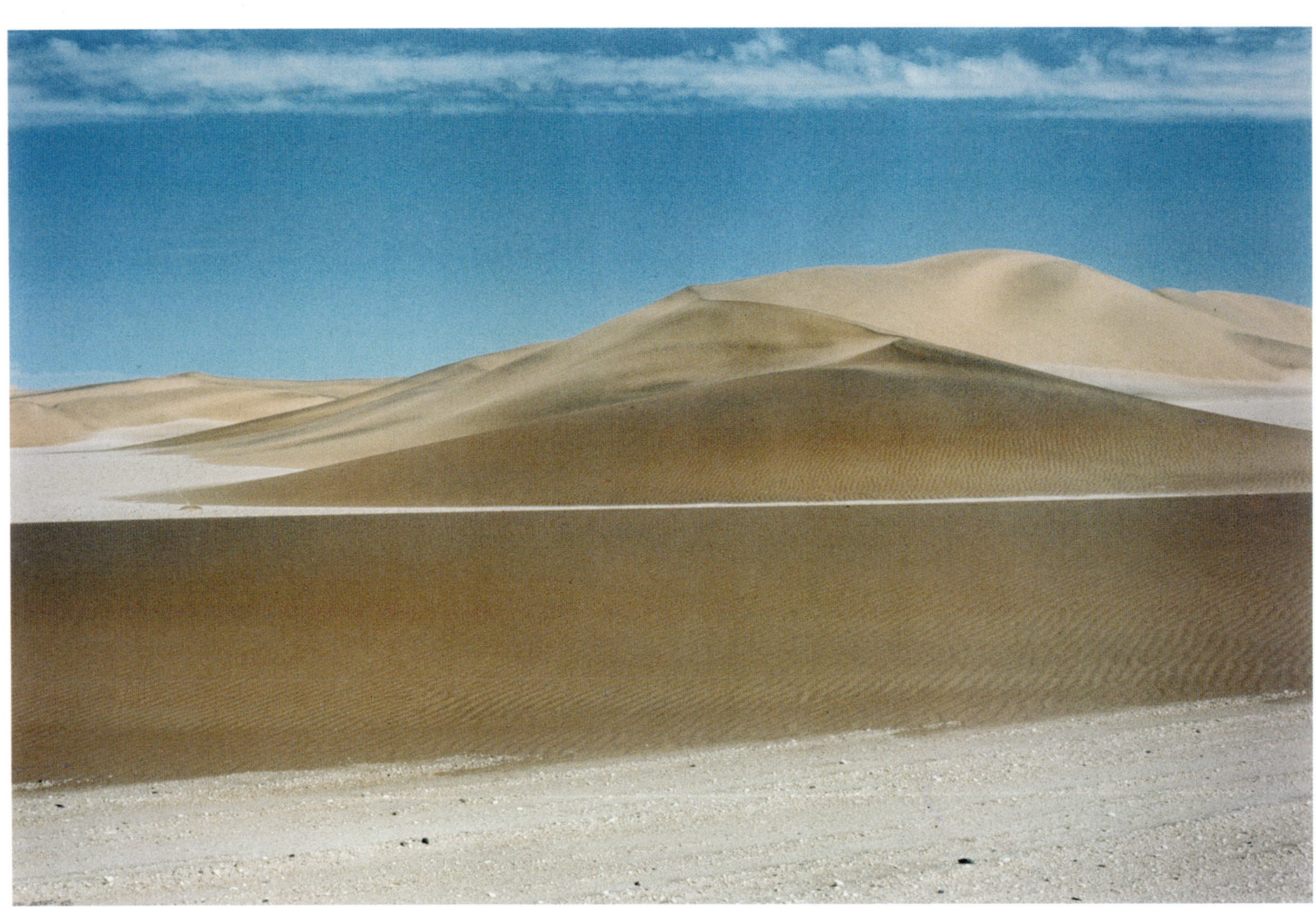

Namib Desert, Namibia 1973

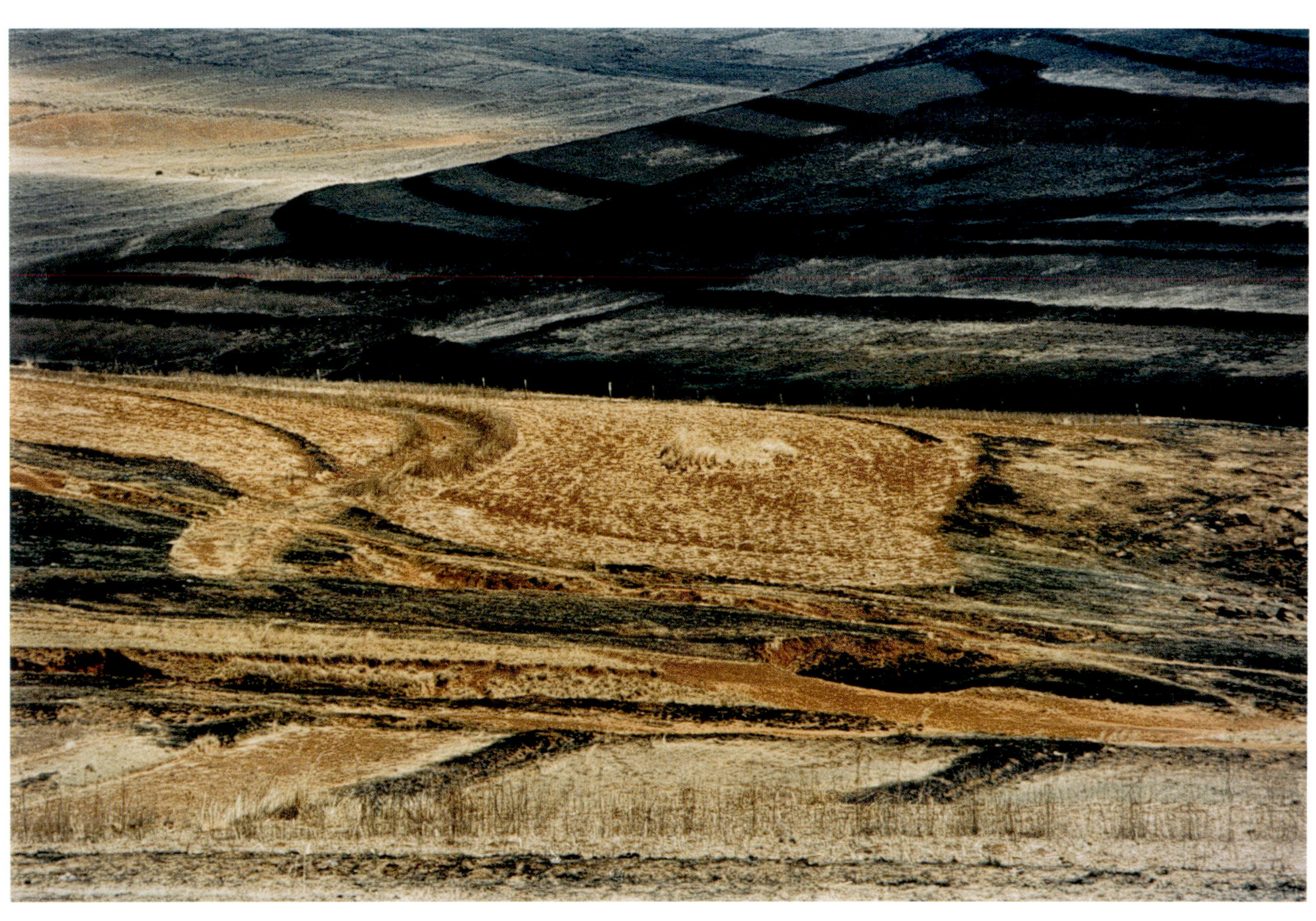

South Africa 1974

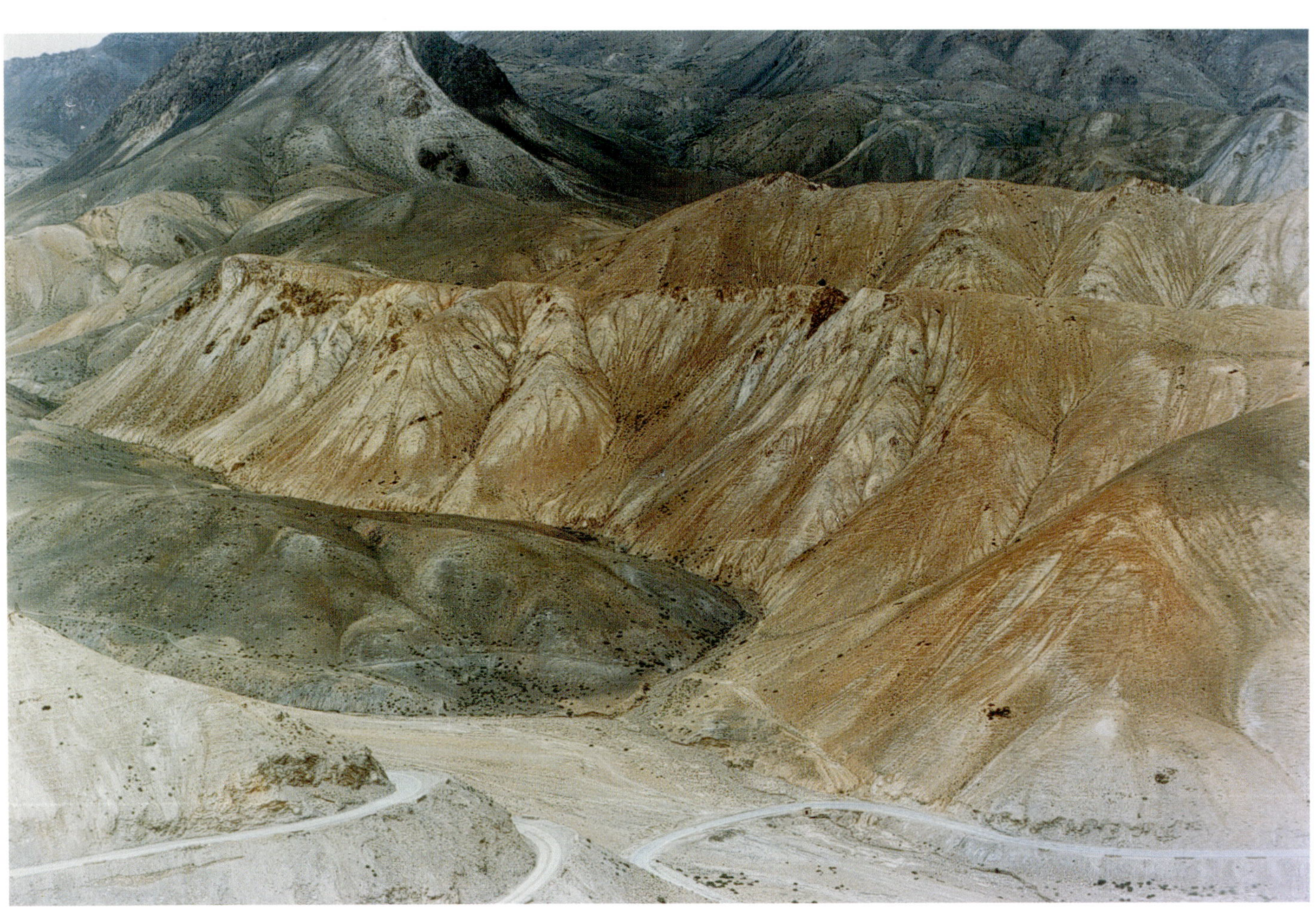

Landscape near Hemis, Ladakh 1976

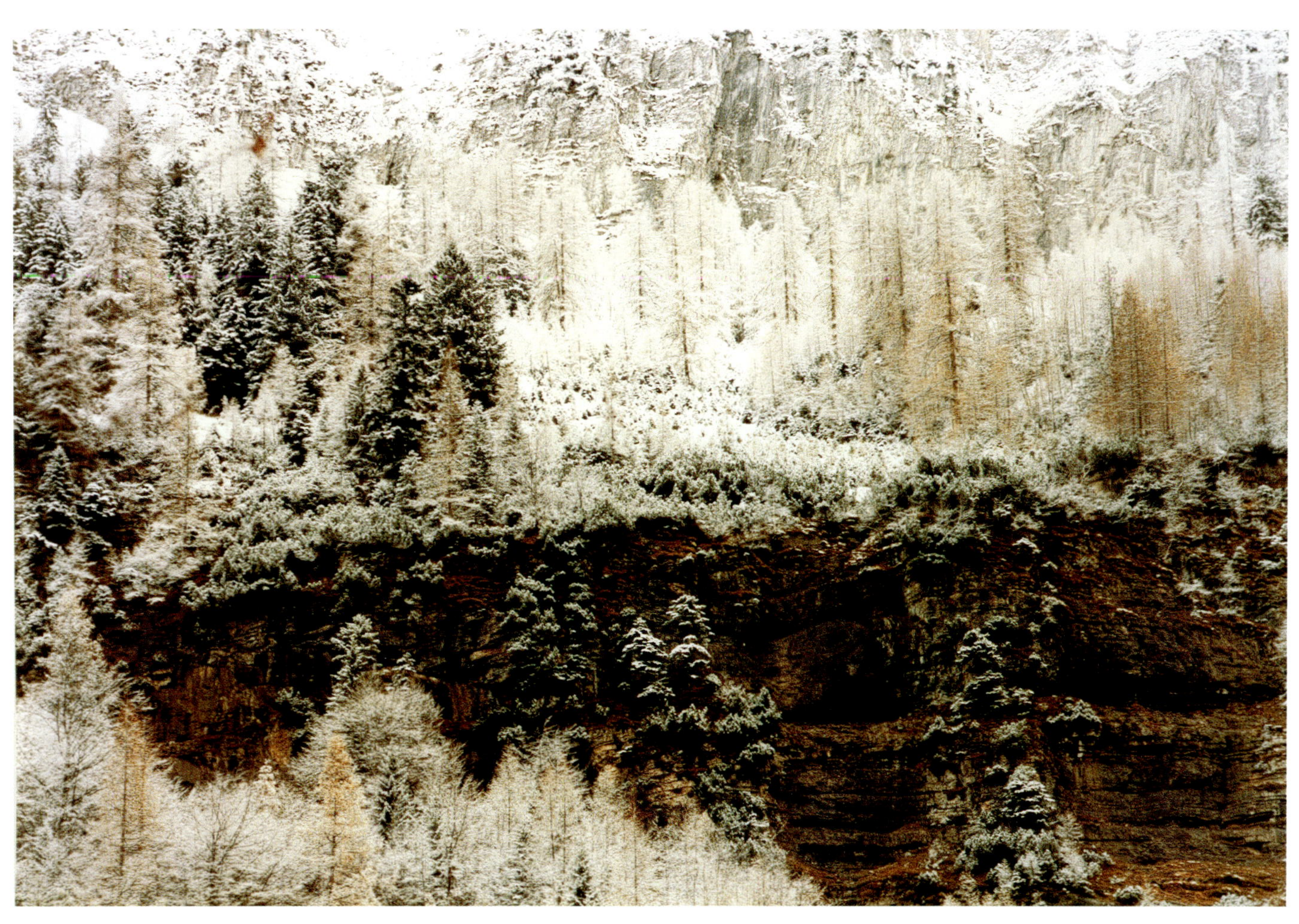

Pfäfers, near Bad Ragaz 1982

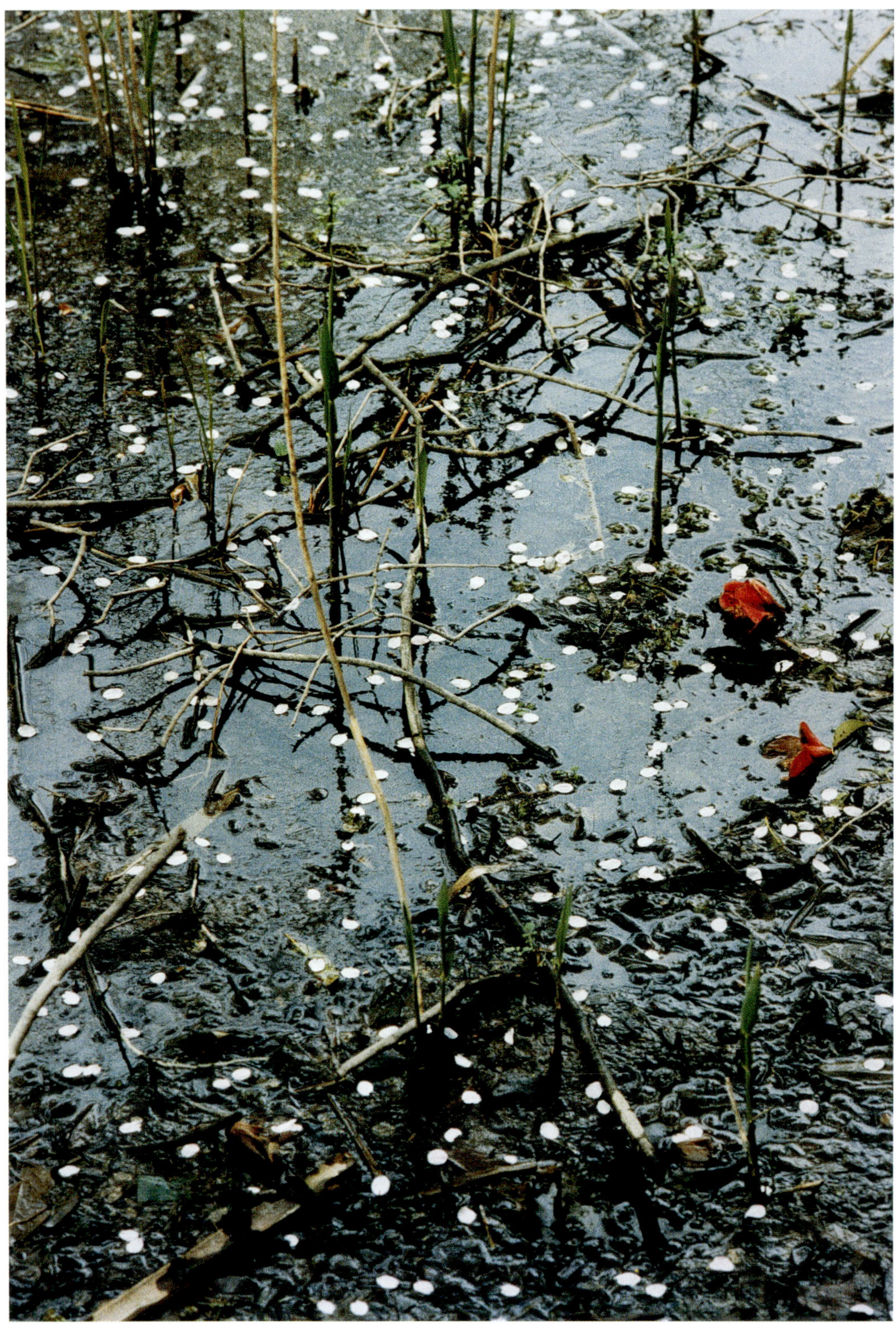

Lake Osana, Near Kyoto 1985

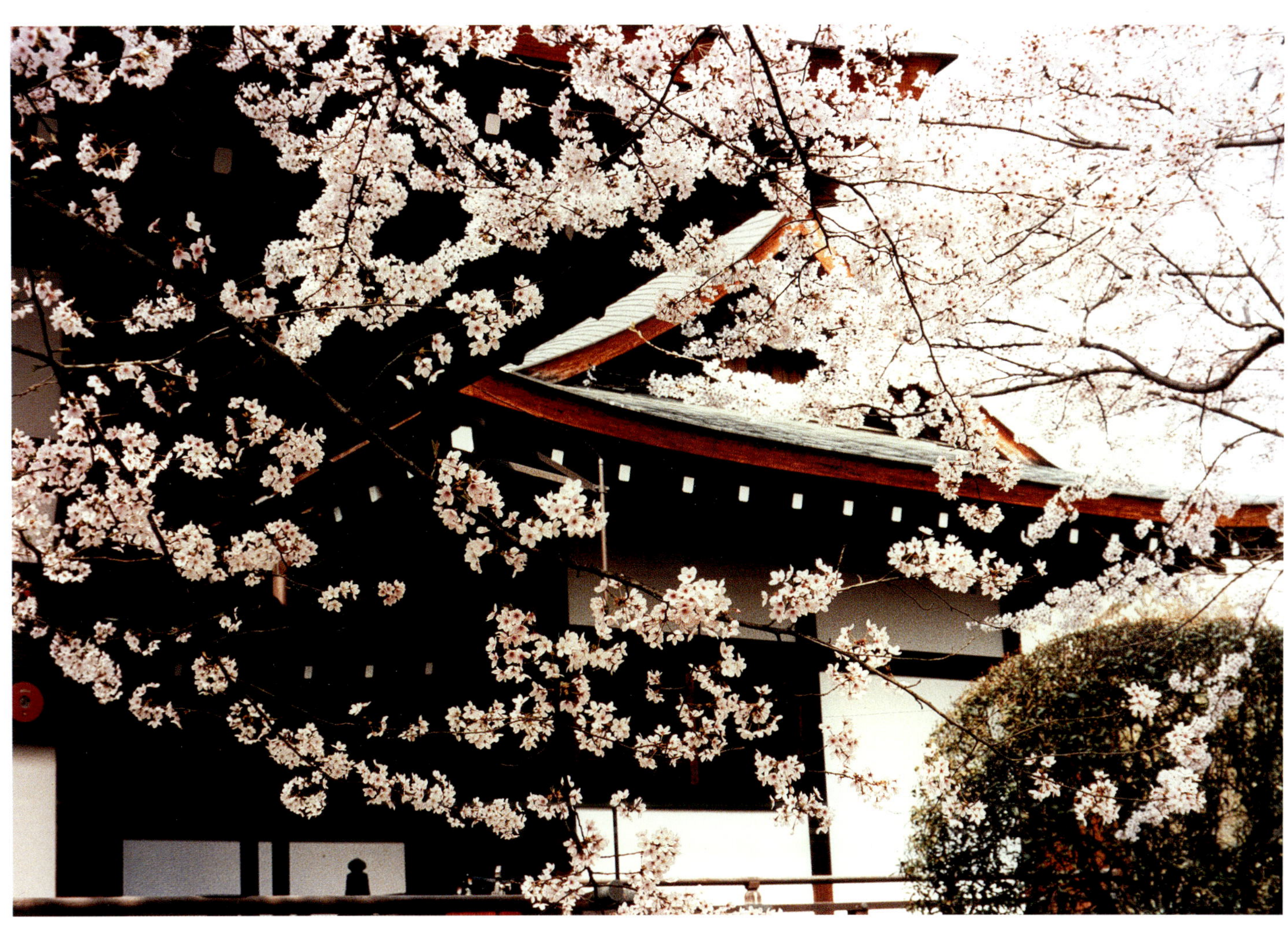

Kyoto, Tenryu-Ji 1985

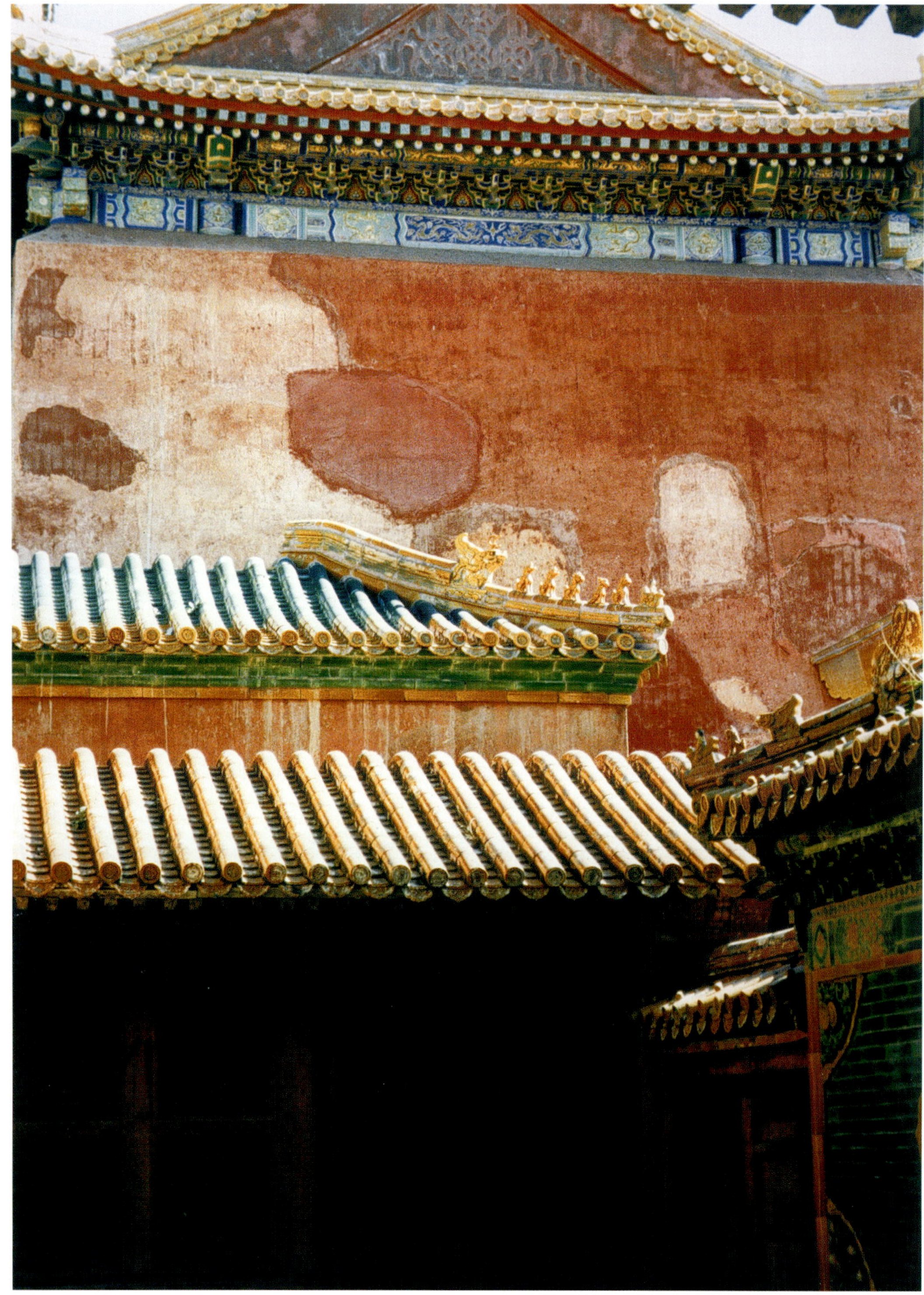

Peking 1990

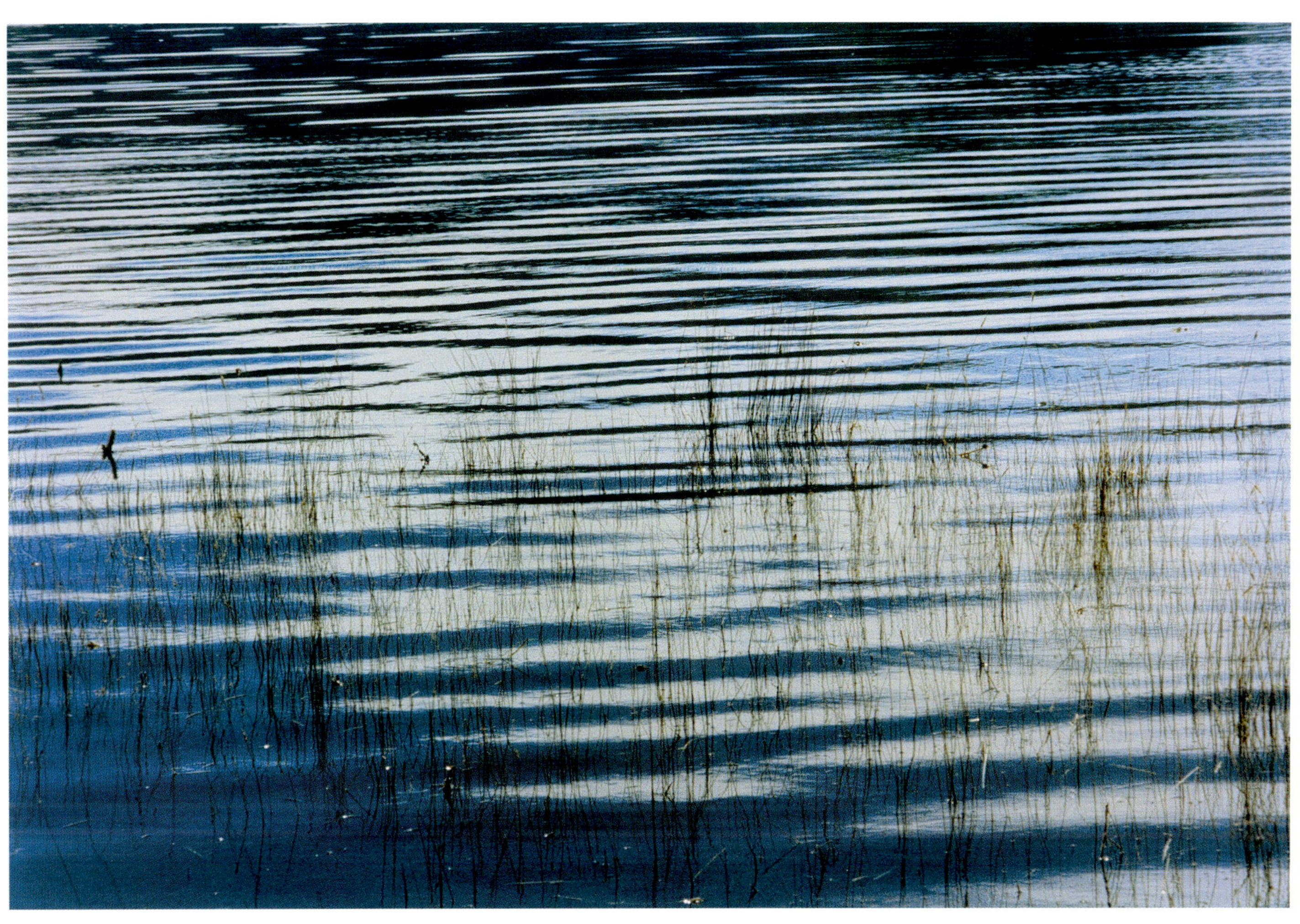

New Zealand 1991

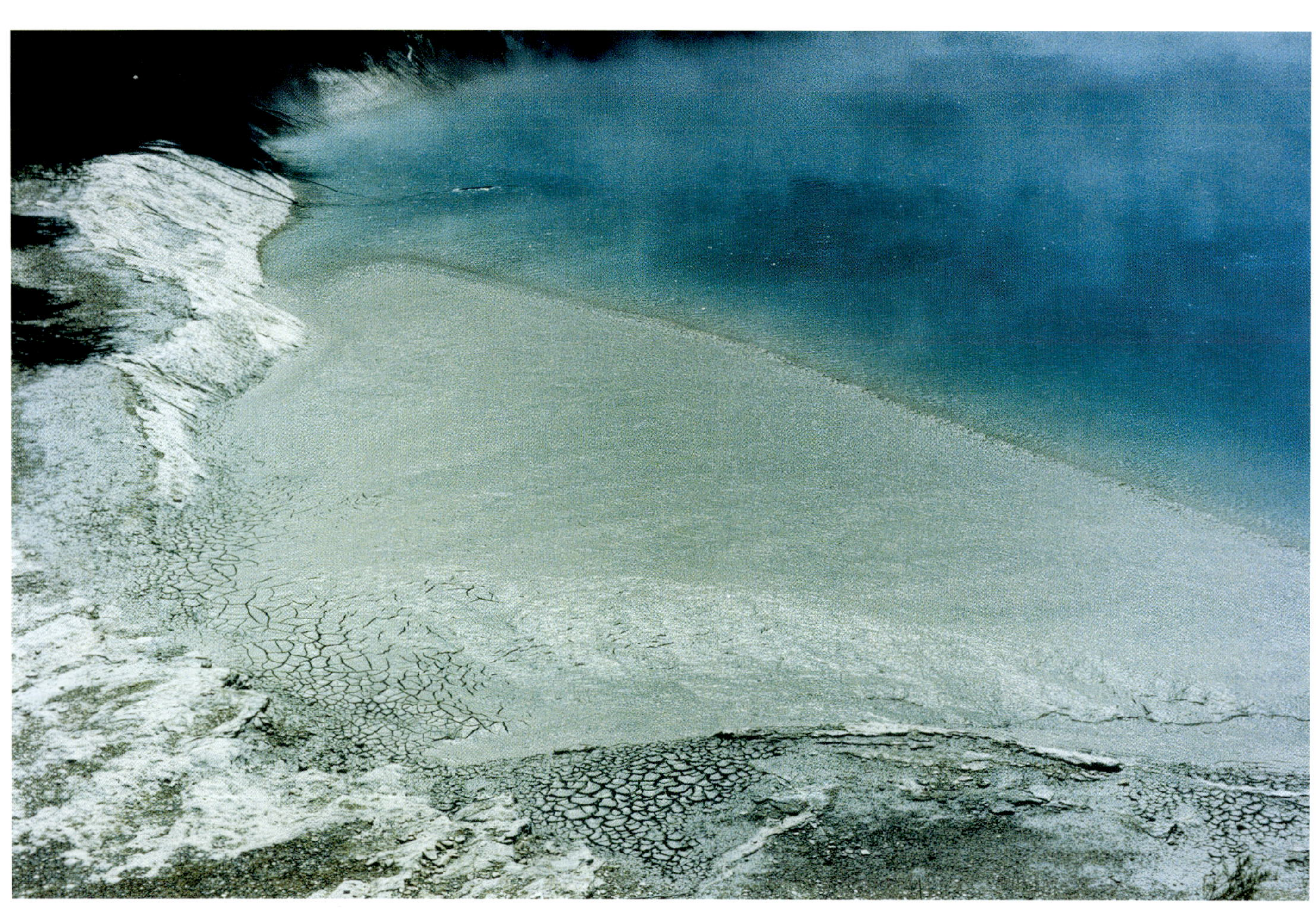

Rotorua, New Zealand 1990

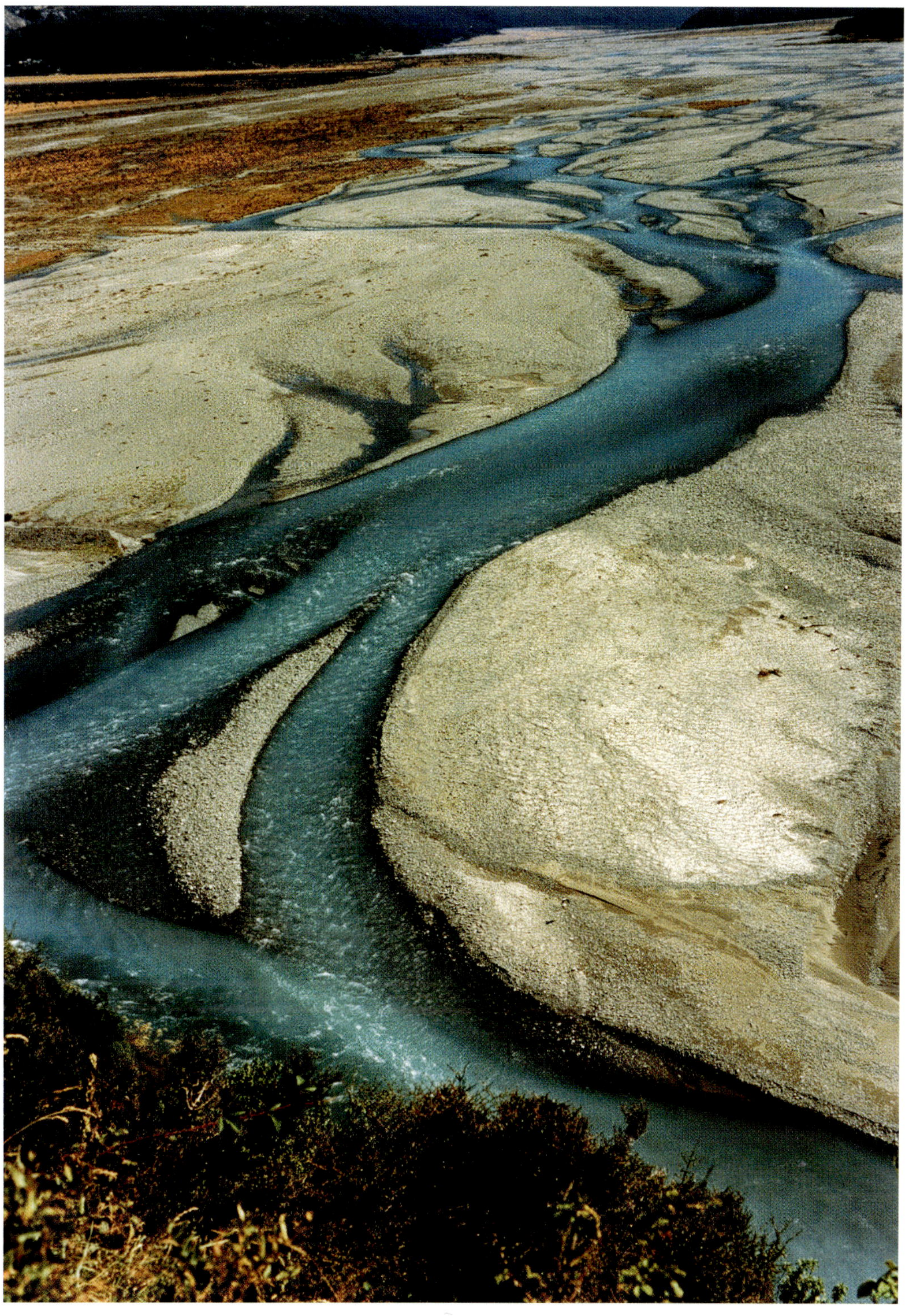

Lewis Pass, New Zealand 1991

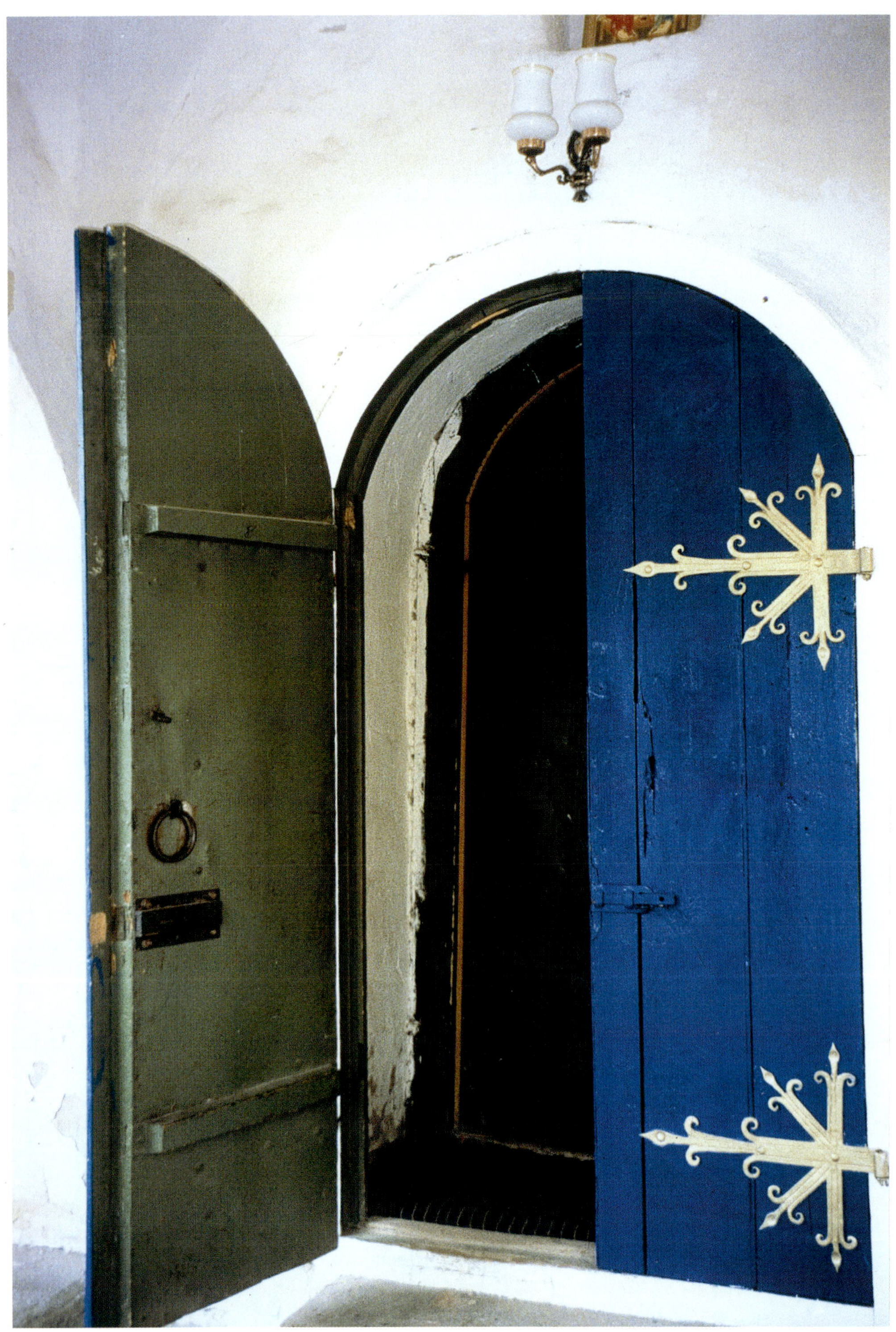

Door in Monastery, Psków   1998